The Chinese Horoscopes Library

TIGER

KWOK MAN-HO

DORLING KINDERSLEY
LONDON • NEW YORK • STUTTGART

A DORLING KINDERSLEY BOOK

Senior Editor Sharon Lucas
Art Editor Camilla Fox
Managing Editor Krystyna Mayer
Managing Art Editor Derek Coombes
DTP Designer Doug Miller
Production Controller Antony Heller
US Editor Laaren Brown

Artworks: Danuta Mayer 4, 8, 11, 17, 27, 29, 31, 33, 35;
Giuliano Fornari 21; Jane Thomson; Sarah Ponder.

Special Photography by Steve Gorton. Thank you to The British Museum, Chinese Post
Office, The Powell-Cotton Museum, Sir Victor Sassoon Chinese Ivories Trust, and The
Board of Trustees of the Victoria & Albert Museum.

Additional Photography: Eric Crichton, Mike Dunning, Jo Foord, Philip Gatward, Steve
Gorton, Dave King, Tim Ridley, Royal Geographical Society.

Picture Credits: Circa Photo Library 13; Courtesy of The Board of Trustees of the Victoria &
Albert Museum 12.

First American Edition, 1994
2 4 6 8 10 9 7 5 3 1

Published in the United States by Dorling Kindersley Publishing, Inc., 95 Madison Avenue,
New York, New York 10016

ISBN 1-56458-611-1
Library of Congress Catalog Number 93-48006

Reproduced by GRB Editrice, Verona, Italy
Printed and bound in Hong Kong by Imago

CONTENTS

Introducing Chinese Horoscopes   8

Casting Your Horoscope 10

Myths and Legends 12

Personality 14

Love 16

Career 18

Health 20

Leisure 22

Symbolism 24

Tiger Standing Still 26

Tiger in the Forest 28

Tiger Passing Through the
Mountains 30

Tiger Going Down the Mountain 32

Tiger Passing Through the Forest 34

Your Chinese Month of Birth ... 36

Your Chinese Day of Birth 38

Your Chinese Hour of Birth 40

Your Fortune in Other Animal
Years 42

Your Chinese Year of Birth ... 44

INTRODUCING CHINESE HOROSCOPES

For thousands of years, the Chinese have used their astrology and religion to establish a harmony between people and the world around them.

The exact origins of the twelve animals of Chinese astrology – the Rat, Ox, Tiger, Rabbit, Dragon, Snake, Horse, Ram, Monkey, Rooster, Dog, and Pig – remain a mystery. Nevertheless, these animals are important in Chinese astrology. They are much more than general signposts to the year and to the possible good or bad times ahead for us all. The twelve animals of Chinese astrology are considered to be a reflection of the Universe itself.

YIN AND YANG

The many differences in our natures, moods, health, and fortunes reflect the wider changes within the Universe. The Chinese believe that every single thing in the Universe is held in balance by the dynamic, cosmic forces of yin and yang. Yin is feminine, watery, and cool; the force of the Moon and the rain. Yang is masculine, solid, and hot; the force of the Sun and the Earth. According to ancient Chinese belief, the concentrated essences of yin and yang became the four seasons, and the scattered essences of yin and yang became the myriad creatures that are found on Earth.

YIN AND YANG SYMBOL
White represents the female force of yin, and black represents the masculine force of yang.

The twelve animals of Chinese astrology are all associated with either yin or yang. The forces of yin rise as Winter approaches. These forces decline with the warmth of Spring, when yang begins to assert

The Little
Red Hen
A Tale of Hard Work

The Little Red Hen
A Tale of Hard Work

Illustrated by Linda Dockey Graves

Adapted by Jennifer Boudart

Publications International, Ltd.

The little red hen lived next to the road by the farmer's house. Where she lived wasn't very fancy, but she loved it. She shared her home with her five baby chicks and her friends, the dog, the cat, and the duck.

The little red hen worked very hard. She kept the house and the yard neat and clean. There was always plenty to do in order to keep everything looking good.

Everyone liked having a clean house and good food on the table. When it came time to do the chores, though, the others always seemed to have something else to do. As soon as the hen would send her baby chicks out to play, the older animals always seemed to disappear, too. The little red hen did all the work herself. Her days were filled with making beds, cleaning, gardening, and cooking.

One day, the little red hen was sweeping her yard. When she looked down on the ground, she found some kernels of wheat. She put the kernels into her pocket for safe keeping. Then she went to look for the dog, cat, and duck. She found them by the pond. She showed them the kernels and asked, "Who will help me plant these?"

Her three friends looked at each other. Then they looked at the little red hen. "Not us," they said. "Right now we need to take a nap."

"I'll plant them myself," she told them. The little red hen returned to the garden and began digging. Soon her baby chicks came to see what she was doing. They told her they wanted to help. The little red hen and her five baby chicks pretended they were burying treasure. The game made the work go quickly.

The little red hen visited the garden every day to watch the wheat grow. She made sure the young plants got plenty of sunshine and care.

One day she found her three friends leaning against the farmer's barn. "There are weeds that are stopping the wheat from growing," said the little red hen. "Will you help me pull the weeds?"

"I can't," said the cat. "The dirt on the weeds would get on my fur. Do you have any idea how long it takes me to wash my paws and tail?"

The dog and the duck both had excuses, too. No one could help. "I'll just do it myself," said the little red hen. Then she walked back to the garden. Once again, her chicks joined her. They had a contest to see who could pull the most weeds. They had fun and finished in no time.

A dry spell kept the rain away for a week. The little red hen was worried about the wheat. If the plants didn't get some water soon, the tender stalks would wither and die. The only thing to do was bring water to the plants. She looked for her friends. She found them on top of the hay pile. "The summer heat is too strong for the wheat. Who will help me water the garden?" asked the little red hen.

The dog, the cat, and the duck looked at her. "We're busy writing a song and can't be bothered now," growled the dog. "Didn't you hear me playing my banjo?"

"I'll just water it myself," she said. The little red hen took her watering pail to the garden. Her chicks kept her company. The hen pretended to be a thundercloud and tried to sprinkle them with water. Before long, the whole garden had been watered.

The wheat grew fast. The little red hen and her chicks lovingly tended to the wheat, and it grew strong and hardy. There was going to be a bumper crop!

Soon it was fall and the wheat turned golden brown. The little red hen knew what that meant. She found her friends playing cards under the farmer's wagon. The hen knelt down and said, "Who will help me harvest the wheat?"

The dog, the cat, and the duck kept their eyes on their cards. "Not us!" they said. "Can't you see we're busy?"

The little red hen stood up and fixed her apron. "I'll harvest it myself," she said. She took her cutting tools to the garden. This time the five chicks were waiting for her. The family cut the wheat and tied it into bundles. They sang songs, and soon the hard work was done.

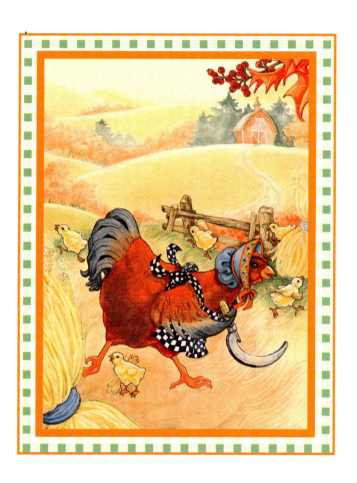

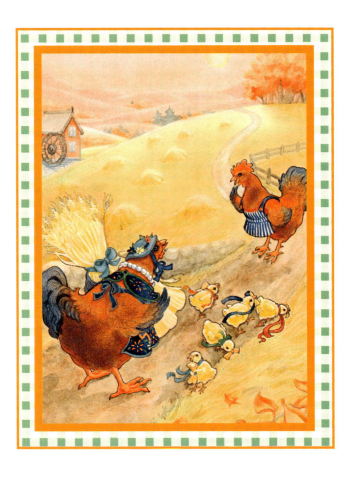

The little red hen knew the work was not finished. She often told her chicks that if a job was worth doing, it was worth doing well.

The little red hen went looking for her friends. She found them sitting by the road. "I need to have the wheat ground into flour," she said. "Who will help me carry it to the miller?"

The dog, the cat, and the duck looked down the road. The miller was located several miles away. "Not us!" the trio said together. "It's too far for us to walk."

Once again, the little red hen would have to do it herself. She and her chicks left right away. It was a long journey, and the chicks moved slowly. The trip seemed to go much faster when they pretended to be hobos traveling with their knapsacks across the country.

The little red hen returned home. She and the chicks were so tired that they quickly fell asleep. The next morning, the little red hen called to her friends who were sunbathing on the roof, "Who will help me bake bread with my flour?"

The dog, the cat, and the duck didn't even look down. "It's a beautiful day. Who would want to be indoors baking bread?" observed the dog.

The hen shook her head. She thought, "Who would want to spend all day doing nothing?" She told the three, "I'll bake it myself." The little red hen went inside. Her chicks tried to make the bread dough for her. Flour was all over the floor and the chicks, too. They shaped the dough into a big loaf and pretended to make a statue. Everyone was sorry to have to stop when the loaf was finished.

The smell of baking bread floated into the air. The dog, the cat, and the duck could smell the tasty treat. They scurried down from the roof and looked into the kitchen through the doorway.

The little red hen had just pulled the warm loaf from the oven. She knew her hard work would be well rewarded by the taste of delicious bread. Her five little chicks danced around her feet.

"Who will help me eat this fresh bread?" asked the little red hen.

"We will!" squeaked the five little chicks.

"We will!" cried the dog, the cat, and the duck from the doorway.

"Well," said the little red hen, "anyone who helped make the bread can have some."

"Yippee!" squeaked the five little chicks. They had helped make the bread.

The dog, the duck, and the cat looked at each other with long faces. The dog's tongue hung hungrily from his mouth. "Can we have just one slice?" he asked as he stared at the warm loaf.

"Anyone who ever helped with the bread can have a slice." said the little red hen. "So, if you helped plant the wheat, water it, weed it, harvest it, take it to the miller, or bake the bread, raise your hand!" Happily, the little chicks put their wings in the air.

The dog, the duck, and the cat looked at the ground. They had never helped the little red hen. They were always too busy having fun.

Later that night, six tummies got their fill of yummy bread as a special reward for work well done. Three other tummies stayed very empty.

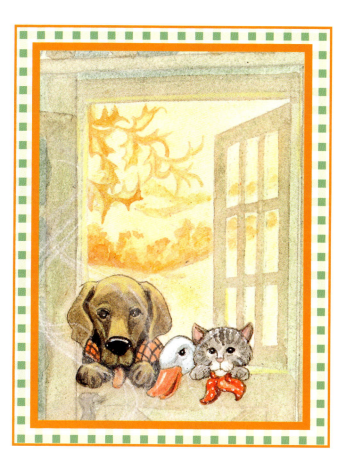

One to Grow On
Hard Work

Play time is always more fun than work time. . . or is it? Think about how the dog, the cat, and the duck in this story spent their days. Now think about how the little red hen and her chicks spent their days. Who do you think had more fun and excitement?

This story shows us that when you work together, you can have fun, too. You also get to enjoy the rewards of your work. How would you rather spend your time?

The End

itself. Even in the course of a normal day, yin and yang are at work, constantly changing and balancing. These forces also naturally rise and fall within us all.

Everyone has their own internal balance of yin and yang. This affects our tempers, ambitions, and health. We also respond to the changes of weather, to the environment, and to the people who surround us.

THE FIVE ELEMENTS

All that we can touch, taste, or see is divided into five basic types or elements – wood, fire, earth, gold, and water. Everything in the Universe can be linked to one of these elements.

For example, the element wood is linked to the Tiger and to the Rabbit. This element is also linked to the color green, sour-tasting food, the season of Spring, and the

emotion of anger. The activity of these elements indicates the fortune that may befall us.

AN INDIVIDUAL DISCOVERY

Chinese astrology can help you balance your yin and yang. It can also tell you which element you are, and the colors, tastes, parts of the body, or emotions that are linked to your particular sign. Your fortune can be prophesied according to the year, month, day, and hour in which you were born. You can identify the type of people to whom you are attracted, and the career that will suit your character. You can understand your changes of mood, your reactions to other places and to other people. In essence, you can start to discover what makes you an individual.

DIVINATION STICKS
Another ancient and popular method of Chinese fortune-telling is using special divination sticks to obtain a specific reading from prediction books.

CASTING YOUR HOROSCOPE

The Chinese calendar is based on the movement of the Moon, unlike the calendar used in the Western world, which is based on the movement of the Sun.

Before you begin to cast your Chinese horoscope, check your year of birth on the chart on pages 44 to 45. Check particularly carefully if you were born in the early months of the year. The Chinese year does not usually begin until January or February, and you might belong to the previous Chinese year. For example, if you were born in 1961 you might assume that you were born in the Year of the Ox. However, if your birthday falls before February 15 you belong to the previous Chinese year, which is the Year of the Rat.

THE SIXTY-YEAR CYCLE

The Chinese measure the passing of time by cycles of sixty years. The twelve animal signs appear five times during the sixty-year cycle, and they appear in a slightly different form every time. For example, if you were born in 1926 you are a Tiger in the Forest, but if you were born in 1938, you are a Tiger Passing Through the Mountains.

MONTHS, DAYS, AND HOURS

The twelve lunar months of the Chinese calendar do not correspond exactly with the twelve Western calendar months. This is because Chinese months are lunar, whereas Western months are solar. Chinese months are normally twenty-nine to thirty days long, and every three to four years an extra month is added to keep approximately in step with the Western year.

One Chinese hour is equal to two Western hours, and the twelve Chinese hours correspond to the twelve animal signs.

The year, month, day, and hour of birth are the keys to Chinese astrology. Once you know them, you can start to unlock your personal Chinese horoscope.

	Water
	Earth		Gold
	Wood		Yin
	Fire		Yang

CHINESE ASTROLOGICAL WHEEL

In the center of the wheel is the yin and yang symbol. It is surrounded by the Chinese astrological character linked to each animal. The band of color indicates your element, and the outer ring reveals whether you are yin or yang.

MYTHS AND LEGENDS

The Jade Emperor, heaven's ruler, asked to see the Earth's twelve most interesting animals. When they arrived, he was impressed by the Tiger's magnificence, and awarded it third place.

The Tiger is associated with courage and bravery. It is reputed to have the power to drive away demons, which is why stone tigers can be found on graves or engraved on doorposts. The Tiger is also known as the protector of children.

The Chinese made sacrifices to the Tiger because it hunted the wild pigs that scavenged on the village fields. Even the Tiger's name suggests the awe in which it was held – it was often referred to as the "king of the mountains."

THE TIGER AND THE DEER

Long ago there lived a small spotted deer. He lived on the edge of a dark forest, but never went in.

However, one day, fierce hunting dogs chased the poor creature into the heart of the forest. He ran and ran until he had lost the hounds, but unfortunately, was also lost himself.

He soon attracted the attention of the other animals of the forest, and they were extremely curious about this intriguing creature. "We've never seen a spotted deer before. How very strange you look," said the animals.

JADE TIGER

This jade paperweight in the shape of a tiger is from China's Sung dynasty (1000–1200).

CHANG TAO LING

This fierce character is Chang Tao Ling, magician, exorcist, and Taoist leader. He rides a tiger to frighten devils and wields the Demon Sword of exorcism.

The next morning the deer wandered into a clearing and suddenly came face to face with an enormous tiger. The deer was terrified and expected the tiger to kill him immediately. But the tiger had never seen such a creature before and was curious. "What kind of creature are you?" asked the tiger, sharpening his claws. "I'm a spotted deer," the deer squeaked.

The tiger was ready to pounce, but he asked another question, "What are those plants growing on your head?" The deer thought quickly and replied, "They are tiger-eating chopsticks."

The tiger was surprised, and said, "You're too small to kill a tiger." "Well, let me tell you," said the deer, "that each of these spots on my body represents a tiger that I have killed." "But if you hunt tigers, why are you shaking with fear?" asked the confused tiger. "Shaking with fear?" said the deer, "Goodness me, no. I am merely building up the energy and force that I need to kill you!"

The tiger did not wait to hear any more and fled into the darkest depths of the forest. The deer, meanwhile, raced off in the opposite direction. Even today, tigers live deep in the forest, hoping to avoid the spotted deer, and spotted deer live on the edge of the forest, hoping to avoid the tiger.

· TIGER ·
PERSONALITY

The Tiger has a competitive and optimistic nature. It is always excited by the possibility of a challenge and has the potential to be a skilled and loyal leader.

You are brave and are rarely afraid to take a physical or intellectual risk. It is most natural for you to follow your instincts, but you also possess self-control and objectivity. You are at your strongest when you have found a fine balance between your sound instincts and innate good judgment.

MOTIVATION
Working for other people is anathema to you. To someone with your excellent leadership qualities, being told what to do is simply too much to endure. It is unlikely to take long, however, before your fighting spirit is recognized, acknowledged, and eventually rewarded.

TIGER FACE
China's Han Dynasty (206BC–AD220) is the period in which this gilded bronze tiger face, now with a slight patina, was made.

Life's comforts are a pleasure for you to enjoy, and financial matters do not cause you great concern. You are sensible and controlled, and never give in to feelings of greed or avarice. Even if your carefully planned investments fail miserably, or if the price of your independence is your job, you invariably respond positively, inventively, or laterally to any challenges. You are often prepared to change your career or profession in order to achieve what you think you deserve.

You are never easily defeated. Instead, you expend your energies on seeking the myriad opportunities that are never too far away.

THE INNER TIGER

Essentially, you have a generous nature, but when you feel threatened or insecure, you tend to withdraw this generosity, and aggression rises to the surface.

If you feel trapped and controlled by people or events, your positive drive is weakened, and the stubborn, quarrelsome aspects of your character begin to predominate. Luckily, this is only a temporary condition, and once your independence and self-respect have been restored, you return quickly to your usual confident self.

In emotional affairs you are intuitive and adventurous. You must be challenged and charmed by your partner, however, for boredom could easily set in.

TIGER-SHAPED WEIGHT

This Chinese tiger-shaped bronze weight derives from the 3rd century BC. Tigers are renowned for their stripes, and this creature is no exception – its precious stripes are inlaid with gold and silver.

Your friendships can be volatile. Although you have the ability to be an exciting and generous friend, you tend to become self-centered when your life runs into difficulties.

THE TIGER CHILD

The young Tiger is honest and has varied interests, but can prove hard to discipline. Parents should try to allow their Tiger child to have space in which to experiment, but it will feel most secure when it knows the extent of its freedom.

· TIGER ·
LOVE

The Tiger is passionate, hasty, and unconventional. It adores the excitement of new love affairs and is likely to have many short-lived relationships.

You are easily swept away by the initial excitement of a new relationship. However, once you have made your conquest, boredom tends to set in, and you are soon ready for a new love affair.

You enjoy a challenge and are attracted to people who are adventurous and independent. You have an extremely excitable nature – even when your heart is broken, you are prepared to bounce back, full of enthusiasm for any relationship.

Ideally, you are suited to the Horse and the Dog. You will admire the Horse's vitality and hardworking nature, and it will let you take

control of situations without ever losing sight of its independence. The Dog's honesty is appealing, and it should prove to be a loyal and protective partner.

The Dragon will introduce a new power and energy into your life, as well as instructing you in worldly wisdom. You and the Ox have vastly different approaches to life, but you could be

GODDESS OF LOVE
Kuan Yin is a powerful figure in Chinese mythology. Once a male Buddhist deity, she is now known as the goddess of mercy, and as Sung-tzu, the giver of children.

CHINESE COMPATIBILITY WHEEL

Find your animal sign, then look for the animals that share its background color – the Tiger has a blue background and is most compatible with the Horse and the Dog. The symbol in the center of the wheel represents double happiness.

happy together if you learn to accept each other's faults. The Rat will be attracted by your inquisitive and passionate nature, but it may try to curb your carefree attitude. You share a sense of independence with the Rabbit, but it is likely to be more restrained in its actions.

Relationships with the Snake, Ram, Monkey, or another Tiger may be difficult. The Snake is too dogmatic and harsh;

ORCHID

In China, the orchid, or Lan Hua, *is an emblem of love and beauty. It is also a fertility symbol and represents many offspring.*

the Ram is too conservative; and the Monkey's cunning and fast pace will eventually undermine you. Two passionate Tigers could easily exhaust each other – another Tiger is likely to be equally enthusiastic about pursuing its own interests, and compromise might be impossible for both of you.

Although the beginning of a relationship with the Rooster may run smoothly, you are soon likely to grow impatient, and it may tire of your constant criticisms.

· TIGER ·
CAREER

The Tiger has excellent organizational skills, and an infectiously positive attitude. It is a strong, enthusiastic leader and is driven by the will to win.

BUSINESS

The world of business is an arena in which the Tiger can use its skills to the fullest. The Tiger thrives on the pressures of meetings and deadlines.

Sometimes it can be dangerously successful in its business dealings, because it is primarily motivated by challenge and risk rather than by the chance to make a profit.

Political rosettes

Watch

Digital diary and address book

POLITICIAN

The Tiger's energy and leadership qualities make it an ideal politician. It is diligent and takes its work seriously. The fear of failure, and the consequent loss of face with its colleagues, only adds to the Tiger's immense drive.

Chinese ivory tiger

EXPLORER

As an explorer, the Tiger can be indomitable. Even when an expedition fails, the Tiger will simply consult its compass and start off again, perhaps in search of beasts similar to this Chinese ivory tiger.

ADVENTURER

Life as an adventurer could suit the Tiger well, since its restless spirit often leads it to seek new experiences. Hot-air ballooning would be a particularly exhilarating adventure, because it contains an attractive element of danger.

Charles Darwin's compass

Modern hot-air balloon

PIONEER

This propeller was made in 1893, by an aviation pioneer. The Tiger loves to be inventive and has a strong pioneering streak.

19th-century propeller

· TIGER ·
HEALTH

Yin and yang are in a continual state of flux within the body. Good health is dependent upon the balance of yin and yang being constantly harmonious.

There is a natural minimum and maximum level of yin and yang in the human body. The body's energy is known as ch'i and is a yang force. The movement of ch'i in the human body is complemented by the movement of blood, which is a yin force. The very slightest displacement of the balance of yin or yang in the human body can lead to poor health. However, yang illness can be cured by yin treatment, and yin illness can be cured

LINGCHIH FUNGUS
The fungus shown in this detail from a Ch'ing dynasty bowl is the "immortal" lingchih fungus, which symbolizes longevity.

by yang treatment. Everybody has their own individual balance of yin and yang. It is likely that a hot-tempered person will have strong yang forces, and that a peaceful person will have strong yin forces. Before Chinese medicine can be prescribed, your moods have to be carefully taken into account. A balance of joy, anger, sadness, happiness, worry, pensiveness, and fear must always be maintained. This fine balance is known in China as the Harmony of the Seven Sentiments.

RHUBARB
The roots and stem of this plant are renowned for their laxative powers.

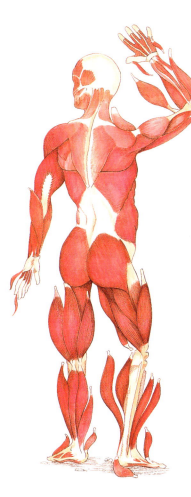

Born in the Year of the Tiger, you are associated with the element wood. This element is linked with the liver, gallbladder, tendons, and eyes. These are the parts of the body that are relevant to the pattern of your health. You are also associated with the emotion of anger and with sour-tasting food.

Rhubarb (*Rheum*) is associated with your Chinese astrological sign. Although it is commonly eaten as a fruit in the Western world, rhubarb is considered extremely toxic in Chinese herbal medicine. However, it is often prescribed for relatively short-term treatment because it is believed to be a very effective stabilizer of the body. It is frequently used to treat ailments such as constipation, coldness in the limbs, and a sinking, slow pulse.

Chinese medicine is highly specific; therefore, never take rhubarb or any other herb unless you are following professional advice from a fully qualified Chinese or Western doctor.

ASTROLOGY AND ANATOMY

Your element, wood, is particularly associated with the liver and the gall-bladder. The liver is a yin organ, and the gallbladder is a yang organ.

· TIGER ·
LEISURE

The Tiger likes to be challenged, even when it is at leisure.
It constantly seeks new and exciting activities, and will
gladly sacrifice its comforts for unexpected adventures.

PICNICKING

The spontaneous nature of picnicking has
great appeal for the Tiger, and it would
particularly enjoy having a sumptuous and
delicious meal during its unexpected
travels. The Tiger also prefers to be
surrounded by objects that are simple and
luxurious. Consequently, this elegant
basket with tea-making equipment would
give it pleasure.

Tea basket

TRAVELING

Model
airplane

Flying and driving are the Tiger's favorite modes
of travel. This 1920s road map set would be the
perfect accessory for the
traveling Tiger.

Leather-cased map set

Chess set

Sheet music

CLASSIC GAMES

Playing chess appeals to the Tiger's love of strategy and its natural competitiveness. One-player puzzles are a solitary pursuit, but the Tiger is quite happy in its own company.

Puzzle

SINGING

The sound of its own voice is a source of pleasure for the Tiger. It is rarely too shy to sing, and is as happy singing on its own as it is leading a large choir.

Porcelain pillow

RELAXING

Taking a break, whether on a luxury item such as this porcelain pillow from the Sung dynasty (1175–1200), or on a simple deck chair, is a valuable and enjoyable pastime for the Tiger.

Deck chair

· TIGER ·
SYMBOLISM

*Each astrological animal is linked with a certain food,
direction, color, emotion, association, and symbol. The
Tiger is also associated with the season of Spring.*

COLOR
*In China, green is the color of
Spring, happiness, and inner
peace. It is also the color that is
associated with the Tiger. A
celadon glaze gives this Chinese
13th- or 14th-century funerary
vase its delicate green color.*

**Chinese vase
with tiger**

FOOD
*There are five tastes according
to Chinese astrology – salty,
acrid, bitter, sour, and sweet.
Sour foods, such as cranberries,
are linked with the Tiger.*

Cranberries

Antique Chinese compass

David Livingstone's compass

DIRECTION

The Chinese compass points south, whereas the Western compass points north. The Tiger's direction is the east.

SYMBOL

The Tiger's symbol in Chinese astrology is the compass.

ASSOCIATION

The field of agriculture is linked with the Tiger.

EMOTION

Anger is the emotion that is connected with the Tiger.

Angry baby

Cereal crops

TIGER STANDING STILL

~ 1914 1974 ~

You are an immensely cautious person and do not willingly take risks. You prefer to remain in safety and security, and you wish to exist in peace and tranquillity.

As a Tiger Standing Still, you are linked to growth, blossoming, and expansion. This signifies that by continuing to work faithfully and doggedly, it is possible for you to rise ever higher in your chosen career, as well as in the esteem of your friends, peers, and associates.

You are linked to the first days of Spring and to the early morning. It is likely, therefore, that you are an early riser and achieve most when the day is young.

Since it is usually the early bird that gets the worm, this sprightliness and natural energy should help you achieve your full potential in your education and your career.

CAREER
In ancient China it was traditionally believed that the natural caution of those born in the year of the Tiger made them the best people to employ in government. This still holds more than an element of truth in the present day, for both male and female Tigers Standing Still are excellent performers in business and management, or in any form of public office.

Your innate caution and wisdom, combined with determination and a certain Tigerish drive to succeed, makes you highly formidable in any committee situation, but firmly reliable as a colleague.

It is likely that your considerable skills will always be in demand at work. As a result, your financial affairs should invariably be healthy and comfortable.

FAMILY
Unfortunately, Tigers Standing Still often have a history of tension with their parents. The reasons for this can be very complex. Sometimes,

Tiger Standing Still

these misunderstandings may occur because your parents do not seem to be treating you as an adult.

A possible solution to this problem is to try to use the naturally cautious approach of the Tiger to your best advantage. This means always finding the time to listen to what your parents are saying, and also giving them sufficient time to listen to your points of view.

Luckily, when you have your own family, you are usually very happy and content. Although your life may sometimes seem to lack excitement, you will invariably feel secure, and enjoy the love and confidence of those around you.

RELATIONSHIPS
All Tigers have a natural tendency to move from one relationship to another. However, as the name suggests, a Tiger Standing Still should be able to avoid this unsettling trait by staying true to itself. There is no reason why you should not be able to enjoy a committed relationship of great stability and fulfillment.

TIGER IN THE FOREST

~ 1926 1986 ~

This Tiger is in its natural habitat. You feel comfortable in any environment, because you have a strong sense of your own self-worth and position in society.

The Chinese have an old saying that the Tiger lives a thousand miles from the city. This refers to the Tiger's independent spirit and wariness, but also hints at an unwillingness to socialize or to take the risk of living close to people. This slightly antisocial tendency is intensified in the Tiger in the Forest.

PERSONALITY

You are linked to the fire and the home, and consequently have the ability to warm or to burn. You are usually very talkative and enjoy the sound of your own voice, but it is sometimes surprisingly valuable to listen to other people, too.

YOUTH

It is likely that you experienced some difficulties during your school years. This should not slow your progress significantly, however, because you are a naturally gifted, hardworking person and should easily catch up with your peers.

FRIENDSHIPS

Your intensified Tiger caution will probably extend to your friendships and also to your relationship with your partner. Although your natural wariness makes you feel more secure, it is not always beneficial for you. Try to learn to trust people more, and allow yourself to be pleasantly enlightened.

You may not always welcome it, but you will probably find that you need another person to help you in your life and in your career. It is best for you to choose this person wisely, since they could open possibilities for you that would not otherwise exist.

Inevitably, you tend to put great personal effort and integrity into whatever you try your hand at,

Tiger in the Forest

proving yourself by the high quality of your work. This will invariably bring you success and should further your many ambitions.

PROSPECTS

You are very intelligent, and your diligent, disciplined approach should mean that you will do well in all aspects of your life. Do not expect instantaneous success, however, for your independent spirit will tend to work against this.

Be prepared to lower your guard, and allow yourself to accept the advice that is most helpful to you. As a result, you should find that life has much to offer, and that you, in return, have much to offer life.

Try not to be frightened or intimidated when you are confronted by challenges, and do not be tempted to avoid them, for these are the situations to which your intelligence is best suited.

When you rise to these various challenges, you are likely to prove yourself and to draw the attention of your colleagues. Consequently, new opportunities are likely to be offered to you, and your life should continue to be fortunate.

TIGER PASSING THROUGH THE MOUNTAINS

~ 1938 1998 ~

*All Tigers are restless and strongly independent, yet
reluctant to take risks. These innate complexities are
intensified in the Tiger Passing Through the Mountains.*

This Tiger is linked to the seemingly contradictory actions of cutting down and blooming. If these contradictions are handled correctly, they can be a considerable strength. Unfortunately, you tend to be stubborn and obstinate and may turn them into a weakness.

PERSONALITY

Your inner turmoil may sometimes lead you to overreact to something of little consequence, or perhaps to treat someone badly for a slight offense. You are prone to extreme swings of mood, which can be as difficult and painful for you to deal with as they are for those who are close to you.

You are invariably tempted to resolve any personal difficulties by quickly moving on to new and unfamiliar situations. Your sense of restlessness usually stems from some inner confusion. You do not necessarily know for sure what you want from life, but that does not stop you from searching for it.

Sometimes you will simply have to take risks; for instance, by trusting other people or by standing by something to the very end. This will invariably be difficult for you, because it goes against your nature – your instincts tell you to run far away when life becomes too precarious, and your natural impatience makes you restless and easily bored.

Remember that risk is not always about putting yourself in danger. Sometimes you will have to take the risk of trusting people enough to let them get close to you. Try this, and you may be pleasantly surprised by the results.

Tiger Passing Through the Mountains

YOUTH

When you were young, you probably had great reserves of energy, and consequently threw yourself into everything around you with enthusiasm. Unfortunately, your severe swings of mood invariably led to various troubles and misunderstandings.

It may often be a good idea for you to move to another town, or even another country, and start life again. But do try to learn from your mistakes, because you cannot run away forever. If you can come to terms with your contradictions, you should eventually be able to become more settled and secure.

RELATIONSHIPS

It is particularly important for you to find a stable partner who can encourage you to accept the consequences of your actions. The security of a committed relationship should be beneficial, for it will help you modify your mood swings and finally face reality.

TIGER GOING DOWN
THE MOUNTAIN

~ 1950 2010 ~

*This is the Tiger with the best of all worlds. You are blessed
with the most auspicious aspects of the Tiger personality
and have virtually unlimited potential.*

You are a very fortunate Tiger, for you are linked to reaping what you have sown and enjoying the fruits of your efforts.

All Tigers are independent and have a tendency to act rashly. You are prone to being flattered and to taking offense too easily.

PERSONALITY
Even though you have your fair share of faults, you are also hardworking and generous, and should establish good relationships at work and in your private life.

Nearly everyone who knows you will put up with your moods, but do not push people too far.

YOUTH
As you grow older, it should become easier for you to cope with your moods. It is likely that your moodiness made school life difficult for you, and consequently, you may not always have shone as brightly as you might have wished.

CAREER
Your early career and financial affairs may be problematic, but do not be disheartened by this slow start. As people come to trust you, and as your friendships offer you more security and support, so you should rise to ever greater authority and financial success.

FRIENDSHIPS
If you try to keep yourself under control, most of your friends and colleagues will see that although you are quick-tempered, you are also forgiving by nature. You wish to restore friendships almost as soon as they have been damaged.

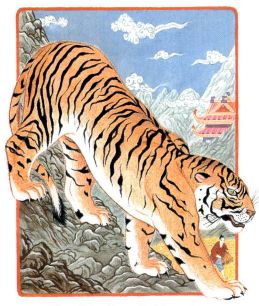

Tiger Going Down the Mountain

RELATIONSHIPS

If you can keep your quick temper under control and do not let yourself become disheartened by early disappointments, you should be able to enjoy a happy and successful committed relationship. The emotional support of this relationship should make you feel more contented and secure.

PROSPECTS

You are associated with the late days of Summer, and it is most likely that you will reap the best rewards for your many endeavors in your late middle age. You have always been an exceedingly fortunate Tiger, and all your tireless, patient hard work should be generously rewarded in the fullness of time.

TIGER PASSING
THROUGH THE FOREST

~ 1902 1962 ~

*This is an aggressive, predatory Tiger. You are linked to a
man carrying a load balanced on a yoke, symbolizing the
need for balance and the risk of fatigue.*

You have considerable potential and a stormy personality. Like a Tiger on the prowl, you are extremely quick in response and often overreact when taken by surprise.

PERSONALITY

When you are confronted with upsetting or disturbing situations, you tend to speak and act immediately, when a wiser person might have paused for thought.

You can, however, turn this weakness into a strength. If you manage to control your natural tendency to quick reactions, you should be valued for your honesty and frankness.

Unfortunately, if left to run riot, this characteristic could lead to trouble. Other people could consider you to be rude, opinionated, and thoughtless.

FEMALE CHARACTERISTICS

The female Tiger Passing Through the Forest is particularly likely to rise to a high position of authority. This is due to the yin influence – it is calming and soothing, and enables the female to balance the different aspects of her personality.

MALE CHARACTERISTICS

The yang influence in the male, however, means that self-control and balance are invariably difficult.

CAREER

It is likely that you did well at school, but the early period of your career may prove difficult. This is usually because people find your torn personality disturbing. If you learn to balance yourself and turn your weaknesses into strengths, life should become much easier.

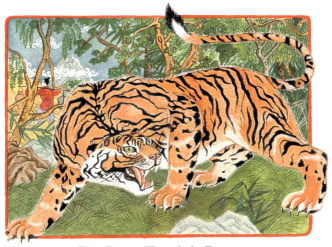

Tiger Passing Through the Forest

RELATIONSHIPS

There are many tensions within your personality, and sometimes it may feel as if you are being torn in opposite directions. Consequently, a committed relationship is often highly problematic, with many arguments and perhaps estrangement from your partner.

Always try to control your quick temper and your sharp tongue. It could be beneficial if you learn to listen to other people and consider their opinions fully. If you can start to achieve some state of balance within yourself, it is highly likely that your committed relationship will eventually become much more stable and rewarding.

CHILDREN

It may take some time before you can work through your inner difficulties and overcome them to any degree. It is therefore probably best for you to have children slightly later in life, when you are much more capable of developing and sustaining close and healthy relationships with them.

YOUR CHINESE
MONTH OF BIRTH

*Find the table with your year of birth, and see where your
birthday falls. For example, if you were born on
August 30, 1950, you were born in Chinese month 7.*

1 You are always optimistic. Try to be more cautious, and learn to make sensible and realistic plans.

2 You are usually overworked and under pressure, but you still manage to be friendly and popular.

3 You are sensitive and are a trusted friend. Emotional matters could be difficult, but stay calm.

4 You were born in the luckiest month in Chinese astrology and should have a very successful life.

5 You are forceful and stubborn, and can be your own worst enemy. Try to learn from your mistakes.

6 You are popular and attractive. Reveal your inner self in order to enjoy a very happy relationship.

7 You are serious, determined, and persistent. You appreciate other people and their needs.

8 You are independent and respected. Beware of envy, and of losing interest in your partner.

9 You are a dedicated follower of fashion, even after your youth. You sometimes lack emotional depth.

10 You can be happy-go-lucky, but are easily exploited. Control any resulting anger and frustration.

11 You are healthy, athletic, and love the great outdoors. Try to slow down in all areas of your life.

12 You are a highly skilled negotiator and invariably achieve your heart's desires.

* Some Chinese years contain double months:	
1914: Month 5	1938: Month 7
May 25 – June 22	July 27 – Aug 24
June 23 – July 22	Aug 25 – Sept 23
1974: Month 4	1998: Month 5
April 22 – May 21	May 26 – June 23
May 22 – June 19	June 24 – July 22

1902	
Feb 8 – March 9	1
March 10 – April 7	2
April 8 – May 7	3
May 8 – June 5	4
June 6 – July 4	5
July 5 – Aug 3	6
Aug 4 – Sept 1	7
Sept 2 – Oct 1	8
Oct 2 – Oct 30	9
Oct 31 – Nov 29	10
Nov 30 – Dec 29	11
Dec 30 – Jan 28 1903	12

1914	
Jan 26 – Feb 24	1
Feb 25 – March 26	2
March 27 – April 24	3
April 25 – May 24	4
* See double months box	5
July 23 – Aug 20	6
Aug 21 – Sept 19	7
Sept 20 – Oct 18	8
Oct 19 – Nov 16	9
Nov 17 – Dec 16	10
Dec 17 – Jan 14 1915	11
Jan 15 – Feb 13	12

1926	
Feb 13 – March 13	1
March 14 – April 11	2
April 12 – May 11	3
May 12 – June 9	4
June 10 – July 9	5
July 10 – Aug 7	6
Aug 8 – Sept 6	7
Sept 7 – Oct 6	8
Oct 7 – Nov 4	9
Nov 5 – Dec 4	10
Dec 5 – Jan 3 1927	11
Jan 4 – Feb 1	12

1938	
Jan 31 – March 1	1
March 2 – March 31	2
April 1 – April 29	3
April 30 – May 28	4
May 29 – June 27	5
June 28 – July 26	6
* See double months box	7
Sept 24 – Oct 22	8
Oct 23 – Nov 21	9
Nov 22 – Dec 21	10
Dec 22 – Jan 19 1939	11
Jan 20 – Feb 18	12

1950	
Feb 17 – March 17	1
March 18 – April 16	2
April 17 – May 16	3
May 17 – June 14	4
June 15 – July 14	5
July 15 – Aug 13	6
Aug 14 – Sept 11	7
Sept 12 – Oct 10	8
Oct 11 – Nov 9	9
Nov 10 – Dec 8	10
Dec 9 – Jan 7 1951	11
Jan 8 – Feb 5	12

1962	
Feb 5 – March 5	1
March 6 – April 4	2
April 5 – May 3	3
May 4 – June 1	4
June 2 – July 1	5
July 2 – July 30	6
July 31 – Aug 29	7
Aug 30 – Sept 28	8
Sept 29 – Oct 27	9
Oct 28 – Nov 26	10
Nov 27 – Dec 26	11
Dec 27 – Jan 24 1963	12

1974	
Jan 23 – Feb 21	1
Feb 22 – March 23	2
March 24 – April 21	3
* See double months box	4
June 20 – July 18	5
July 19 – Aug 17	6
Aug 18 – Sept 15	7
Sept 16 – Oct 14	8
Oct 15 – Nov 13	9
Nov 14 – Dec 13	10
Dec 14 – Jan 11 1975	11
Jan 12 – Feb 10	12

1986	
Feb 9 – March 9	1
March 10 – April 8	2
April 9 – May 8	3
May 9 – June 6	4
June 7 – July 6	5
July 7 – Aug 5	6
Aug 6 – Sept 3	7
Sept 4 – Oct 3	8
Oct 4 – Nov 1	9
Nov 2 – Dec 1	10
Dec 2 – Dec 30	11
Dec 31 – Jan 28 1987	12

1998	
Jan 28 – Feb 26	1
Feb 27 – March 27	2
March 28 – April 25	3
April 26 – May 25	4
* See double months box	5
July 23 – Aug 21	6
Aug 22 – Sept 20	7
Sept 21 – Oct 19	8
Oct 20 – Nov 18	9
Nov 19 – Dec 18	10
Dec 19 – Jan 16 1999	11
Jan 17 – Feb 15	12

YOUR CHINESE
DAY OF BIRTH

*Refer to the previous page to discover the beginning of your
Chinese month of birth, then use the chart below to
calculate your Chinese day of birth.*

If you were born on May 5, 1902,
your birthday is in the Chinese
month starting on April 8. Find 8
on the chart below. Using 8 as the
first day, count the days until you
reach the date of your birthday.
(Remember that not all months
contain 31 days.) You were born
on day 28 of the Chinese month.

If you were born in a Chinese
double month, simply count the days
from the first date of the month that
contains your birthday.

1	2	3	4	5	6	7
8	9	10	11	12	13	14
15	16	17	18	19	20	21
22	23	24	25	26	27	28
29	30	31				

DAY 1, 10, 19, OR 28
You are trustworthy and set high
standards, but tend to rush your

projects. Try to be cautious, and do
not be too self-obsessed. You may
receive unexpected money but must
control your spending. You are
suited to a career in the public sector
or the arts.

DAY 2, 11, 20, OR 29
You are honest and popular. You
need peace, but also require lively
company. You are prone to
outbursts of temper. You tend to
enjoy life and make the most of your
opportunities. You are suited to a
literary or artistic career.

DAY 3, 12, 21, OR 30
You are quick-witted, but may
appear to be difficult. As a result,
people may be wary of being your
friend. You have a disciplined
character and fight for the truth. You
are suited to careers that have a
competitive element.

Day 4, 13, 22, or 31

You are very warmhearted, but also have a reserved attitude, which can sometimes make you appear unapproachable. If you try to be more outgoing and sociable, you should become more popular. You have a calm and patient manner, and are suited to a career as an academic or researcher.

Day 5, 14, or 23

Your fiery, obstinate nature can sometimes make it difficult for you to accept suggestions or opinions from others, and your stubbornness may lead to quarrels or problems. You should be lucky with money and may often use your profits to set up new projects. Your innate intelligence will enable you to cope with a demanding career.

Day 6, 15, or 24

You have an open, stable, and cheerful character, and enjoy an active social life. You are affectionate and emotional, and have a tendency to daydream. This can lead to confusion, and your eagerness to help others may be stifled by your indecision. Although you will never be wealthy, you should always have enough money.

Day 7, 16, or 25

You enjoy a certain amount of excitement in your life, but must learn to become more realistic and disciplined. Although you are a natural performer, you should beware of alienating your friends or colleagues. In your career, the opportunity to travel is more important to you than a good salary or a high standard of living.

Day 8, 17, or 26

You have very good judgment, but should not act too quickly. Your social skills may sometimes be lacking, and you may alienate other people, so try to be more tactful. You will experience poverty, but also wealth. Your calm and determined nature is combined with a free spirit, making you best suited to self-employment.

Day 9, 18, or 27

You are happy, optimistic, and warmhearted. You keep yourself busy and are rarely troubled by trivialities. Occasionally you quarrel unnecessarily with your friends, and it is important for you to learn to control your moods. You are particularly suited to a career as a sole owner or proprietor.

YOUR CHINESE
HOUR OF BIRTH

In Chinese time, one hour is equal to two Western hours.
Each Chinese double hour is associated with one of the
twelve astrological animals.

11 P.M. – 1 A.M. RAT HOUR
You are independent and have a hot temper. Try to think before you speak. Your thrifty nature will be useful in business and at home. You are willing to help those who are close to you, and they will return your support.

1 – 3 A.M. OX HOUR
Up to the age of twenty, your life could be difficult, but your fortunes are likely to improve after these troublesome years. In your career, be prepared to take a risk or to leave home during your youth to achieve your goals. You should enjoy a prosperous old age.

3 – 5 A.M. TIGER HOUR
You have a lively and creative nature, which may cause family arguments in your youth. Between the ages of twenty and forty you may have many problems. Luckily, your fortunes are likely to improve dramatically in your forties.

5 – 7 A.M. RABBIT HOUR
Your parents should be helpful, but your siblings may be your rivals. You may have to move away from home to achieve your full potential at work. Your committed relationship may take time to become settled, but you should get along much better with everyone after middle age.

7 – 9 A.M. DRAGON HOUR
You have a quick-witted, determined, and attractive nature. Your life will be busy, but you could sometimes be lonely. You should achieve a good standard of living. Try to curb your excessive self-confidence, for it could make working relationships difficult.

9 – 11 A.M. SNAKE HOUR
You have a talent for business and should find it easy to build your career and provide for your family. You have a very generous spirit and will gladly help your friends when they are in trouble. Unfortunately, family relationships are unlikely to run smoothly.

11 A.M. – 1 P.M. HORSE HOUR
You are active, clever, and obstinate. Try to listen to advice. You are fascinated with travel and with changing your life. Learn to control your extravagance, for it could lead to financial suffering.

1 – 3 P.M. RAM HOUR
Steady relationships with your family, friends, or partners are difficult, because you have an active nature. You are clever, but must not force your views on others. Your fortunes will be at their lowest in your middle age.

3 – 5 P.M. MONKEY HOUR
You earn and spend money easily. Your character is attractive, but frustrating, too. Sometimes your parents are not able to give you adequate moral support. Your committed relationship should be good, but do not brood over emotional problems for too long – if you do your career could suffer.

5 – 7 P.M. ROOSTER HOUR
In your teenage years you may have many arguments with your family. There could even be a family division, which should eventually be resolved. You are trustworthy, kind, and warmhearted, and never intend to hurt other people.

7 – 9 P.M. DOG HOUR
Your brave, capable, hard-working nature is ideally suited to self-employment, and the forecast for your career is excellent. Try to control your impatience and vanity. The quality of your life is far more important to you than the amount of money you have saved.

9 – 11 P.M. PIG HOUR
You are particularly skilled at manual work and always set yourself high standards. Although you are warmhearted, you do not like to surround yourself with too many friends. However, the people who are close to you have your complete trust. You can be easily upset by others, but are able to forgive and forget quickly.

YOUR FORTUNE IN OTHER ANIMAL YEARS

*The Tiger's fortunes fluctuate during the twelve animal years.
It is best to concentrate on a year's positive aspects, and to
take care when faced with the seemingly negative.*

YEAR OF THE RAT
This is likely to be a year of difficulty. At times, there may seem to be no escape – you will be confronted with problems both at home and at work. However, as long as you keep yourself calm, all should eventually go well in the Year of the Rat.

YEAR OF THE OX
Although you are likely to suffer some form of illness during the Year of the Ox, this is nevertheless a good year for the Tiger. Once you have recovered your strength and your spirits, you should be able to enjoy success in many areas of your life.

YEAR OF THE TIGER
Unfortunately, your own year is likely to be full of hardship. Your finances will be stretched, and there is likely to be illness and perhaps even death in your family. Try not to let this affect your family relationships.

YEAR OF THE RABBIT
You should find yourself at an advantage for much of the Year of the Rabbit. It is also likely to be a particularly good year for your family life. The only shadow on the immediate horizon is the possibility of accidents outside the home.

YEAR OF THE DRAGON
This is a difficult year. Your finances are likely to be stretched, and the Year of the Dragon is also likely to bring illness, and even death, to distant relatives. Try not to allow these difficulties to affect your relationship with your family.

YEAR OF THE SNAKE

 This year contains various negative elements, such as illness and difficulties. Luckily, the Year of the Snake also contains positive elements, and if you are determined and persevere, you should be able to enjoy a certain degree of success.

YEAR OF THE HORSE

 Your career and your family life should run smoothly. However, you must beware of people's jealousy, in both professional and personal spheres. Jealousy is dangerous, because it could spoil areas of your life that you value highly.

YEAR OF THE RAM

 Learn to take sufficient care of your physical and mental health in the Year of the Ram. It is a particularly auspicious time to use any opportunities that you are offered. You should be able to enjoy success in many areas of your life this year.

YEAR OF THE MONKEY

 You will be given many opportunities this year. Unfortunately, you will also be given many trials and will therefore feel confused and unsettled for most of the year. Nothing will be achieved if you get upset, so do your best to stay calm.

YEAR OF THE ROOSTER

 Try to retain a positive outlook this year. The Year of the Rooster is an intriguing time for the Tiger, and even though the year may have a dismal start, various areas of your life should turn out to your advantage.

YEAR OF THE DOG

 There may be new additions to your family this year. The Year of the Dog is an excellent year with many opportunities, especially for work abroad. However, other people could become jealous of your good fortune, so be careful.

YEAR OF THE PIG

 Beware, for the Year of the Pig could be a dangerous year for you, and you should take particular care of your health. Various areas of your life are likely to be unsettled this year, and you must always try to be on guard.

YOUR CHINESE
YEAR OF BIRTH

*Your astrological animal corresponds to the Chinese year of
your birth. It is the single most important key in the quest
to unlock your Chinese horoscope.*

Find your Western year of birth in
the left-hand column of the chart.
Your Chinese astrological animal is
on the same line as your year of birth
in the right-hand column of the
chart. If you were born in the
beginning of the year, check the

middle column of the chart carefully.
For example, if you were born in
1963, you might assume that you
belong to the Year of the Rabbit.
However, if your birthday falls
before January 25, you actually
belong to the Year of the Tiger.

1900	Jan 31 – Feb 18, 1901	Rat
1901	Feb 19 – Feb 7, 1902	Ox
1902	Feb 8 – Jan 28, 1903	Tiger
1903	Jan 29 – Feb 15, 1904	Rabbit
1904	Feb 16 – Feb 3, 1905	Dragon
1905	Feb 4 – Jan 24, 1906	Snake
1906	Jan 25 – Feb 12, 1907	Horse
1907	Feb 13 – Feb 1, 1908	Ram
1908	Feb 2 – Jan 21, 1909	Monkey
1909	Jan 22 – Feb 9, 1910	Rooster
1910	Feb 10 – Jan 29, 1911	Dog
1911	Jan 30 – Feb 17, 1912	Pig
1912	Feb 18 – Feb 5, 1913	Rat
1913	Feb 6 – Jan 25, 1914	Ox
1914	Jan 26 – Feb 13, 1915	Tiger
1915	Feb 14 – Feb 2, 1916	Rabbit
1916	Feb 3 – Jan 22, 1917	Dragon

1917	Jan 23 – Feb 10, 1918	Snake
1918	Feb 11 – Jan 31, 1919	Horse
1919	Feb 1 – Feb 19, 1920	Ram
1920	Feb 20 – Feb 7, 1921	Monkey
1921	Feb 8 – Jan 27, 1922	Rooster
1922	Jan 28 – Feb 15, 1923	Dog
1923	Feb 16 – Feb 4, 1924	Pig
1924	Feb 5 – Jan 23, 1925	Rat
1925	Jan 24 – Feb 12, 1926	Ox
1926	Feb 13 – Feb 1, 1927	Tiger
1927	Feb 2 – Jan 22, 1928	Rabbit
1928	Jan 23 – Feb 9, 1929	Dragon
1929	Feb 10 – Jan 29, 1930	Snake
1930	Jan 30 – Feb 16, 1931	Horse
1931	Feb 17 – Feb 5, 1932	Ram
1932	Feb 6 – Jan 25, 1933	Monkey
1933	Jan 26 – Feb 13, 1934	Rooster

Year	Dates	Animal	Year	Dates	Animal
1934	Feb 14 – Feb 3, 1935	Dog	1971	Jan 27 – Feb 14, 1972	Pig
1935	Feb 4 – Jan 23, 1936	Pig	1972	Feb 15 – Feb 2, 1973	Rat
1936	Jan 24 – Feb 10, 1937	Rat	1973	Feb 3 – Jan 22, 1974	Ox
1937	Feb 11 – Jan 30, 1938	Ox	1974	Jan 23 – Feb 10, 1975	Tiger
1938	Jan 31 – Feb 18, 1939	Tiger	1975	Feb 11 – Jan 30, 1976	Rabbit
1939	Feb 19 – Feb 7, 1940	Rabbit	1976	Jan 31 – Feb 17, 1977	Dragon
1940	Feb 8 – Jan 26, 1941	Dragon	1977	Feb 18 – Feb 6, 1978	Snake
1941	Jan 27 – Feb 14, 1942	Snake	1978	Feb 7 – Jan 27, 1979	Horse
1942	Feb 15 – Feb 4, 1943	Horse	1979	Jan 28 – Feb 15, 1980	Ram
1943	Feb 5 – Jan 24, 1944	Ram	1980	Feb 16 – Feb 4, 1981	Monkey
1944	Jan 25 – Feb 12, 1945	Monkey	1981	Feb 5 – Jan 24, 1982	Rooster
1945	Feb 13 – Feb 1, 1946	Rooster	1982	Jan 25 – Feb 12, 1983	Dog
1946	Feb 2 – Jan 21, 1947	Dog	1983	Feb 13 – Feb 1, 1984	Pig
1947	Jan 22 – Feb 9, 1948	Pig	1984	Feb 2 – Feb 19, 1985	Rat
1948	Feb 10 – Jan 28, 1949	Rat	1985	Feb 20 – Feb 8, 1986	Ox
1949	Jan 29 – Feb 16, 1950	Ox	1986	Feb 9 – Jan 28, 1987	Tiger
1950	Feb 17 – Feb 5, 1951	Tiger	1987	Jan 29 – Feb 16, 1988	Rabbit
1951	Feb 6 – Jan 26, 1952	Rabbit	1988	Feb 17 – Feb 5, 1989	Dragon
1952	Jan 27 – Feb 13, 1953	Dragon	1989	Feb 6 – Jan 26, 1990	Snake
1953	Feb 14 – Feb 2, 1954	Snake	1990	Jan 27 – Feb 14, 1991	Horse
1954	Feb 3 – Jan 23, 1955	Horse	1991	Feb 15 – Feb 3, 1992	Ram
1955	Jan 24 – Feb 11, 1956	Ram	1992	Feb 4 – Jan 22, 1993	Monkey
1956	Feb 12 – Jan 30, 1957	Monkey	1993	Jan 23 – Feb 9, 1994	Rooster
1957	Jan 31 – Feb 17, 1958	Rooster	1994	Feb 10 – Jan 30, 1995	Dog
1958	Feb 18 – Feb 7, 1959	Dog	1995	Jan 31 – Feb 18, 1996	Pig
1959	Feb 8 – Jan 27, 1960	Pig	1996	Feb 19 – Feb 6, 1997	Rat
1960	Jan 28 – Feb 14, 1961	Rat	1997	Feb 7 – Jan 27, 1998	Ox
1961	Feb 15 – Feb 4, 1962	Ox	1998	Jan 28 – Feb 15, 1999	Tiger
1962	Feb 5 – Jan 24, 1963	Tiger	1999	Feb 16 – Feb 4, 2000	Rabbit
1963	Jan 25 – Feb 12, 1964	Rabbit	2000	Feb 5 – Jan 23, 2001	Dragon
1964	Feb 13 – Feb 1, 1965	Dragon	2001	Jan 24 – Feb 11, 2002	Snake
1965	Feb 2 – Jan 20, 1966	Snake	2002	Feb 12 – Jan 31, 2003	Horse
1966	Jan 21 – Feb 8, 1967	Horse	2003	Feb 1 – Jan 21, 2004	Ram
1967	Feb 9 – Jan 29, 1968	Ram	2004	Jan 22 – Feb 8, 2005	Monkey
1968	Jan 30 – Feb 16, 1969	Monkey	2005	Feb 9 – Jan 28, 2006	Rooster
1969	Feb 17 – Feb 5, 1970	Rooster	2006	Jan 29 – Feb 17, 2007	Dog
1970	Feb 6 – Jan 26, 1971	Dog	2007	Feb 18 – Feb 6, 2008	Pig